Afro-Cuban
Coordination For Drumset

by Maria Martinez

PLAYBACK+
Speed • Pitch • Balance • Loop

To access audio visit:
www.halleonard.com/mylibrary

Enter Code
7854-3216-0324-7137

Edited by Rick Mattingly

ISBN 978-0-7935-9749-9

7777 W. BLUEMOUND RD. P.O. BOX 13819 MILWAUKEE, WI 53213

Visit Hal Leonard Online at
www.halleonard.com

ACKNOWLEDGMENTS AND DEDICATION

I am very grateful to have had the opportunity to live in and become a citizen of the United States of America. This experience was realized through the valiant courage and determination of my parents, Isabel and Miguel Martinez, who left Cuba and arrived in the United States as refugees with three young children (myself and two sisters). Traveling to a foreign land, leaving family behind, and learning a new language were just a few of the many challenges faced by my parents. It is with great pride and respect that I dedicate this book to my parents and to the bravery of all Cuban-American refugees.

A very special thanks to my family for their endless love and support: Isabel Martinez and Miguel Martinez, Maria, Jorge, Angelica and Amanda Gonzalez, Teresa, Bobby, Bobby Jr. and Coleen Castello, Juan Garcia, Robin Wright and the Wright family.

Thanks to all my endorsers for the great equipment and continued support over the years: Paiste, Latin Percussion, Regal Tip, Remo, Rhythm Tech, E-Pad, and Pearl Drums.

Special thanks to Rick Mattingly for his hard work and excellent editing on this book, *Brazilian Coordination for Drumset*, and *The Instant Guide to Drum Grooves*. I truly appreciate your patience, professionalism, and friendship. Thanks to Jeff Schroedl, Greg Herriges, and the staff at Hal Leonard for making this project possible.

AUDIO CREDITS

Drumset, Maracas, Clave: Maria Martinez; **Bass, Guiro:** George Lopez; **Keyboards:** Cheche Alara (tracks 7–10 and 13–36), Carlos Cuevas (tracks 1–6 and 11–12) **Sax:** Robert Kyle; **Conga, Bongo, Shekere:** Danny Reyes; **Engineer:** Bob Nagy. Recorded at The Note Well Studio. Produced by Maria Martinez.

ABOUT THE AUTHOR

Maria Martinez was born in Camaguey, Cuba and raised in New Orleans, Louisiana. She has studied drumset and percussion with Joe Porcaro, Joey Barron, Casey Scheuerell, Ralph Humphrey, Alex Acuna, Steve Houghton, Alan Dawson, and many others.

Martinez is the author of several educational publicatins, including the book/audio and videos *Brazilian Coordination for Drumset* and *Afro-Cuban Coordination for Drumset*, and *The Instant Guide to Drum Grooves* book/ audio (published by Hal Leonard Corporation).

Maria is a respected drummer, percussionist, clinician, and educator. She has taught master classes, conducted clinics, and played at events such as PASIC (Percussive Arts Society International Convention), NAMM (National American Music Merchants), and TCAP (The California Arts Project), to name a few.

Martinez pursues an active freelance career, performing and sharing stage and studio with such artists as Barry White, El Chicano, Angela Bofill, Rita Coolidge, Nel Carter, Klymaxx, Emmanuel, Johnny Paycheck, Trini Lopez, and others. Her television and recording appearances include The Late Show, Soul Train, Klymaxx' *Good Loving* music video, The Drew Carey Show, Dukes of Hazzard, and Pearl's *No Borders* CD.

CONTENTS

AUDIO TRACKS

In order to assist you in developing the proper "feel" for the Afro-Cuban rhythms covered in this book, the accompanying compact disc features demonstration and play-along tracks that can be used when practicing the ostinatos, patterns and exercises. Ostinatos that are demonstrated on the audio are identified with the corresponding track number inside a black diamond next to the written example.

3+2 Mambo

◆1 Demo, half note = 80
(p.28, #3)

◆2 Play-along, half note = 80

◆3 Demo, half note = 90
(p.9, #3)

◆4 Play-along, half note = 90

◆5 Demo, half note = 100
(p.28, #1)

◆6 Play-along, half note = 100

2+3 Mambo

◆7 Demo, half note = 80
(p.9, #4)

◆8 Play-along, half note = 80

◆9 Demo, half note = 90
(p.19, #10)

◆10 Play-along, half note = 90

◆11 Demo, half note = 100
(p.19, #5)

◆12 Play-along, half note = 100

3+2 Nañigo

◆13 Demo, dotted quarter note = 110
(p.65, #1)

◆14 Play-along, dotted quarter note = 110

◆15 Demo, dotted quarter note = 120
(p.65, #3)

◆16 Play-along, dotted quarter note = 120

◆17 Demo, dotted quarter note = 130
(p.65, #2)

◆18 Play-along, dotted quarter note = 130

3+2 Songo

◆19 Demo, half note = 100
(p.69, #6)

◆20 Play-along, half note = 100

◆21 Demo, half note = 112
(p.69, #5)

◆22 Play-along, half note = 112

◆23 Demo, half note = 126
(p.69, #2)

◆24 Play-along, half note = 126

2+3 Songo

◆25 Demo, half note = 100
(p.69, #8)

◆26 Play-along, half note = 100

◆27 Demo, half note = 112
(p.69, #3)

◆28 Play-along, half note = 112

◆29 Demo, half note = 126
(p.69, #10)

◆30 Play-along, half note = 126

2+3 Mozambique

◆31 Demo, half note = 100
(New York style)

◆32 Play-along, half note = 100

◆33 Demo, half note = 110
(New York style)

◆34 Play-along, half note = 110

◆35 Demo, half note = 120
(New York style)

◆36 Play-along, half note = 120

Clave

◆37 Play-along, 2+3 son clave

◆38 Play-along, 3+2 son clave

◆39 Play-along, 2+3 rumba clave

◆40 Play-along, 3+2 rumba clave

INTRODUCTION

Although the drumset has never been a traditional part of the Mambo, Mozambique, and Nanigo styles, adaptations by contemporary "Latin-jazz" drummers has made these styles (as well as the Songo style) popular with many drumset players. The patterns in *Afro-Cuban Coordination for Drumset* are hybrid rhythms from the Afro-Cuban styles as applied to the drumset, and are often played in Latin-jazz settings. The book also includes extensive material devoted to mastering the ability to play the clave pattern with the left foot on hi-hat or via a pedal mounted to a cowbell or Jam Block — a technique that has become increasingly popular with many drumset players.

Afro-Cuban Coordination for Drumset will enable you to develop the necessary coordination with which to play in a variety of Afro-Cuban musical styles. By combining ostinatos with coordination studies and variations, the book provides challenging material for drummers. But *Afro-Cuban Coordination for Drumset* goes beyond just teaching mechanics. The book is filled with rhythmic phrases typical of the Afro-Cuban style that will help you make the transition from practicing coordination exercises to playing music.

The accompanying audio contains demo and play-along tracks in the Mambo, Songo, Mozambique, and Nanigo styles, along with Clave tracks in the 2+3 and 3+2 rumba and son claves. Practicing with the play-along track will help you get the feel of the rhythmic style and also help you learn to lock in with other musicians.

In addition to practicing the material in this book, you must listen to these styles. Learning a particular musical style includes becoming acquainted with all aspects of the style you intend to learn and play. A selected discography of Afro-Cuban music is included that you can use as a starting point. Listen to the ways in which the drums, percussion, bass, piano, etc. interact with each other.

Because there are so many ways to play and interpret Afro-Cuban music, I encourage you to check out other Afro-Cuban books that include drumset patterns, percussion parts, and musical history. To learn the "language" of the Afro-Cuban style and its drumming, familiarize yourself with the feel of the music, the traditional percussion instruments used in the music, and the traditional parts played on those instruments.

It is my sincere hope that this book will provide you with an effective and musical way to acquire all the coordination you need in order to express your musical ideas with ease.

— *Maria Martinez*

RECOMMENDED LISTENING

Afrocuba: *Rey Arco Iris* (Caribe Productions 9460) 1996. Afro-Cuban Jazz

Justo Almario: *Count Me In* (Intergrity 8942) 1995. Latin Jazz

Ray Barretto: *Ancestral Messages* (Picante/Concord 4549) 1993. Latin Jazz

Batacumbele: *En Aquellos Tiempos* (Disco Hit 1693) 1991. Latin Jazz/Songo

Michel Camilo: *Thru My Eyes* (Tropijazz 82067) 1997. Latin Jazz

Caribbean Jazz Project: *Island Stories* (Heads Up 3039) 1997. Latin Jazz

Luis Conte: *La Cocina Caliente* (Denon 30001, Import) Latin Jazz

Cuban All-Stars: *Pasaporte: Tata Guines & Miguel Anga* (Enja 9019) 1995. Afro-Cuban Jazz

Cubanismo!: *Malembe* (Hannibal 1411, Import) 1997. Afro-Cuban Jazz

Paquito D'Rivera: *CubaJazz: Featuring Bebo & Chucho Valdez* (Tropijazz 82016) 1996. Latin Jazz

Clare Fischer: *Tjaderama* (Discovery 551) 1992. Latin Jazz

Dizzy Gillespie: *Dizzy's Diamonds: The Best of the Verve Years* (3-CD set, Verve/Poly. 13875) Latin Jazz

Jerry Gonzalez & Fort Apache Band: *Moliendo Cafe* (Sunnyside 1061) 1992. Latin Jazz

Roy Hargrove: *Crisol Habana* (Verve/Poly. 537563) 1997. Latin Jazz

Conrad Herwig: *The Latin Side Of John Coltrane* (Astor Place 4003) 1996. Latin Jazz

Giovanni Hidalgo: *Worldwide* (RMM/Sony 81056) 1993. Latin Jazz

Irakere: *The Best Of Irakere* (Columbia/Sony 57719) 1994. Latin Jazz

Orlando Valle "Maraca" Y Otra Vision: *Sonando!* (Ahi-Nama Records 1018) 1998. Afro-Cuban Jazz

Chico O'Farrill: *Chico O'Farrill & his Afro-Cuban Jazz Orchestra: Pure Emotion* (Milestone 9239) 1995. Big Band Mambo Jazz

Eddie Palmieri: *Palmas* (Elektra 961649) 1994. Latin Jazz

Charlie Parker: *South Of The Border* (Verv/Poly. 527 779) Latin Jazz

Carlos "Patato" Valdes: *Masterpiece* (Messidor 15827-2) 1993. Latin Jazz

Pello El Afrokan: *Un Sabor Que Canta* (Vitral 4122, Import) 1989. Congas and Comparsas

Danilo Perez: *Danilo Perez* (Novus/BMG 63148) 1993. Latin Jazz

Tito Puente: *No Hay Mejor* (Tico 1401) 1975. Big Band Mambo Jazz

Humberto Ramirez: *Portrait Of A Stranger* (Tropijazz 81685) 1995. Latin Jazz

Gonzalo Rubalcaba: *Diz...Gonzalo Rubalcaba Trio* (Blue Note 30490) 1995. Latin Jazz

Hilton Ruiz: *Hands On Percussion* (Tropijazz 81483) 1995. Latin Jazz

Steve Turre: *Steve Turre* (Verve/Poly. 537133) 1997. Latin Jazz.

Various Artists: *Best of Latin Jazz* (Verve/Poly.314 517 956-2) 1993. Latin Jazz

Various Artists: *Fiesta Picante: The Latin Jazz Party Collection* (2-CD Set, Picante/Concord 4782) 1997. Latin Jazz

CLAVE

The Cuban clave is a two-bar rhythmic phrase — one bar with three notes and the other bar with two notes, hence referred to as "3+2 clave" or "forward clave." To change the direction of the clave, simply reverse the two bars, resulting in "2+3 clave" or "reverse clave." Typically, the rhythmic feel or melody of a song will determine the direction of the clave.

The rhythmic foundation of most Cuban music is based around the clave. All instruments in the ensemble play musical phrases in accordance to the clave's direction and rhythmic feel. Once the clave pattern begins in a song (in either 2+3 or 3+2) it typically does not change direction, unless the arrangement has a section or phrase with an odd number of bars.

There are two types of Cuban clave: son clave and rumba clave. Folkloric Cuban musical styles typically use rumba clave; son clave is generally used more in Cuban dance styles.

Both claves originally derived from the 6/8 clave where it is felt and played with a triple feel. As time went on, the clave evolved into a duple feel, which is felt and played in 2/4 or 2/2. It is important to feel the half-note pulse while playing clave in 2/2, the quarter-note pulse in 2/4, and the dotted-quarter-note pulse in 6/8. The pulse can also be felt in one when the tempo is fast or when triple and duple meters need to be felt and implied simultaneously.

NOTATION KEY

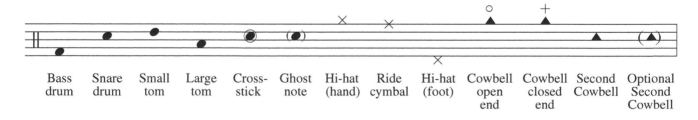

| Bass drum | Snare drum | Small tom | Large tom | Cross-stick | Ghost note | Hi-hat (hand) | Ride cymbal | Hi-hat (foot) | Cowbell open end | Cowbell closed end | Second Cowbell | Optional Second Cowbell |

Chapter 1: MAMBO

Mambo is a term that loosely describes the style we are referring to in this section. In Cuban music, the tempo can sometimes distinguish one particular style from another, and the Mambo style is generally played at fast tempos. The audio tracks will help you acquire the correct feel and provide you with slow, medium and fast tempos in which to play.

Although the drumset has never traditionally been part of the Mambo style, contemporary drummers have adapted the rhythms played on traditional percussion instruments in this popular style. The traditional ensemble generally utilizes congas, timbales, guiro, claves, bongos/bell, bass, piano, horns and vocals.

The following page contains basic Mambo patterns with 3+2 and 2+3 clave patterns, played by a cross-stick on the snare drum, along with the tumbao figure that is played on the bass drum in the Mambo style and variations for the left-foot hi-hat. The cymbal pattern is the standard "cascara" pattern — a two-bar phrase that can be played in 2+3 or 3+2 son or rumba clave. The literal translation for the word "cascara" is "shell." This is the pattern traditionally performed by the timbale player on the side or shell of the timbale or on a mambo bell. Drumset players can play it on ride cymbal, cowbell (mambo bell), closed hi-hat, or on the side (shell) of the floor tom. When using a mambo bell, play the accents on the open end and the other notes on the body of the cowbell.

Following the page with the basic Mambo/cascara patterns are several pages showing ride-cymbal (or mambo bell) variations in the four different clave feels. These can all be played with the different bass drum/hi-hat patterns from the patterns on page 9. Typically, a Latin-jazz drummer will play the standard two-bar cascara pattern on hi-hat or the shell of the floor tom during the A section of a standard AABA-style tune, and play a two-bar variation on ride cymbal or cowbell during the B section or "bridge." Variations are also frequently used during solo sections. This corresponds to what the timbale player would do in a traditional Afro-Cuban song.

Begin by playing a pattern from page 9 and then play a two-bar variation in the same clave, alternating between the two patterns. Patterns 1–3 on page 9 correspond with variation page 10; patterns 4–6 correspond with variation page 12; patterns 7–9 correspond with variation page 14; patterns 10–12 correspond with variation page 16. After each page of variations there is a summary page that combines many of the variation patterns. Individual lines of the summaries can be practiced and played as 4-bar phrases.

Before attempting to play each exercise on the drumset, you may find it very helpful to sing the cascara pattern and each ride cymbal (or mambo bell) variation while clapping the clave rhythm. This will help you internalize the clave and play each variation with a better feel. Choose two different syllables to sing: one for the accented notes and one for the unaccented notes. Sing both syllables with a short sound. Clap the clave rhythm and repeat the cascara pattern and each variation as needed before combining the two phrases. Do the same with each summary.

3+2 Son Clave

1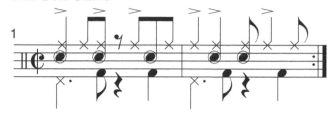

3+2 Rumba Clave

7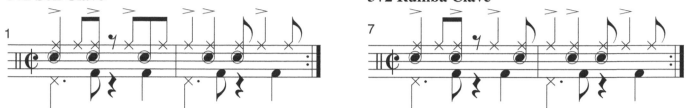

2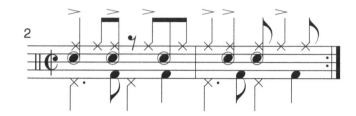

8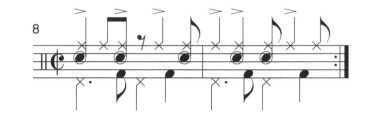

3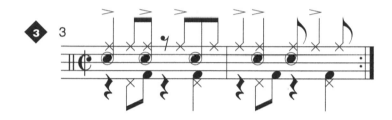

9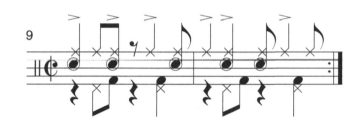

2+3 Son Clave

4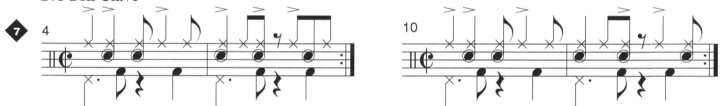

2+3 Rumba Clave

10

5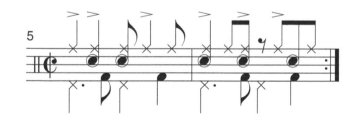

11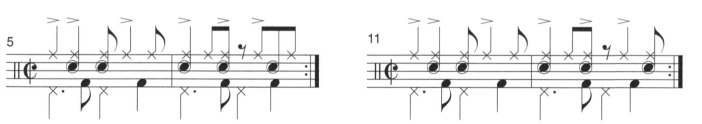

6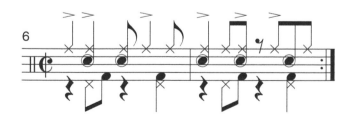

12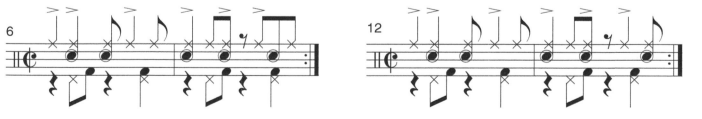

RIDE CYMBAL VARIATIONS, 3+2 Rumba Clave

14

Chapter 2: MAMBO VARIATIONS

The following Mambo patterns involve the left hand playing a cross-stick snare drum note on the "and" of one in each cut-time bar, and a tom-tom note (or two) on the "and" of two, which replaces the bass drum note. Even though the clave is not being played, it must always be felt, and it is still reflected in the cascara pattern played on the ride cymbal or mambo bell.

Following the basic Mambo patterns on page 19 are several pages showing ride-cymbal (or mambo bell) variations in the four different clave feels, which can be substituted for the cascara pattern shown in the examples on page 19. Typically, a drummer will play the standard two-bar cascara pattern on the hi-hat or the shell of the floor tom during the A section of a standard AABA-style tune, and play a two-bar variation on ride cymbal or cowbell during the B section or "bridge." Variations are also frequently used during solo sections. When playing the variations on a mambo bell, play the accented notes on the open end and the other notes on the body of the cowbell.

Begin by playing a pattern from page 19 and then play a two-bar ride-cymbal (or mambo bell) variation, alternating between the two patterns. Patterns 1–3 on page 19 correspond with variation page 20; patterns 4–6 correspond with variation page 22; patterns 7–9 correspond with variation page 24; patterns 10–12 correspond with variation page 26. After each page of variations, a summary page combines many of the variation patterns. Individual lines from the summaries can be practiced and played as 4-bar phrases.

Before attempting to play each basic pattern, variation and summary with the Mambo audio tracks, play them with tracks 37–40, which contain only the clave pattern. This will help you internalize the clave and play each variation with a better feel.

3+2 Son or Rumba Clave

1

2
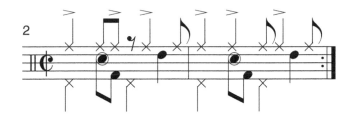

3
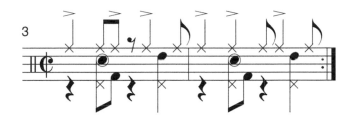

2+3 Son or Rumba Clave

4

5
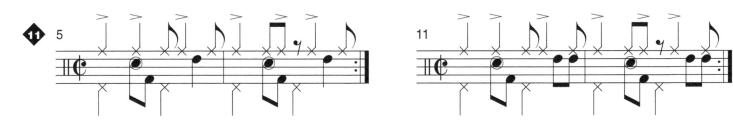

6
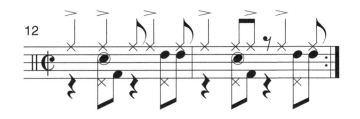

3+2 Son or Rumba Clave

7
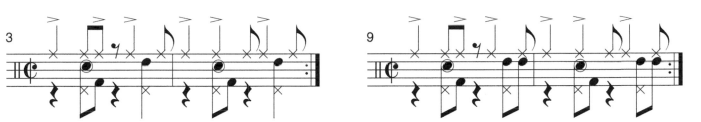

8
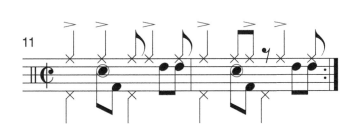

9
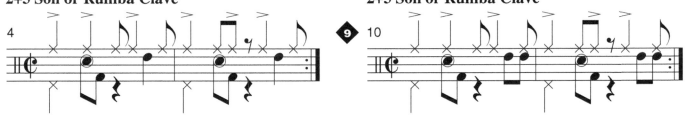

2+3 Son or Rumba Clave

10
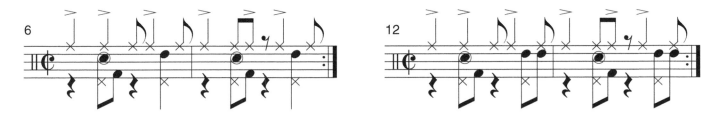

11
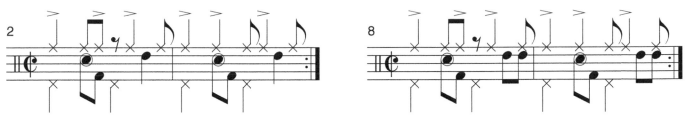

12
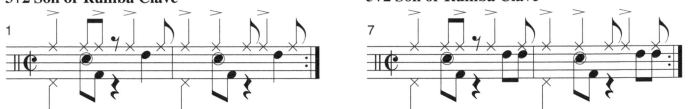

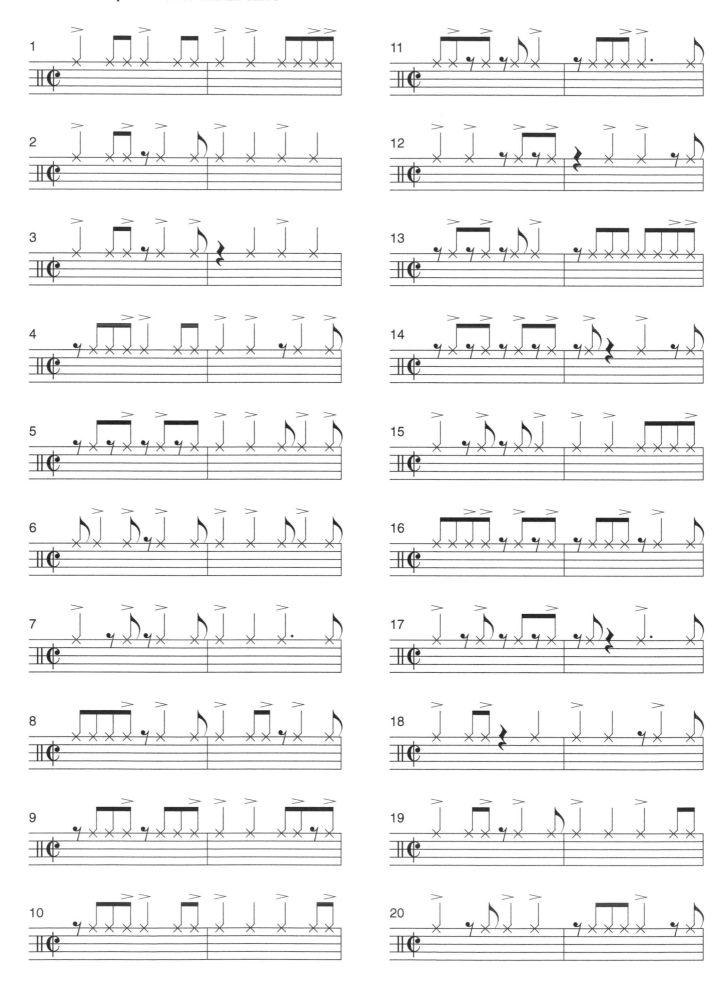

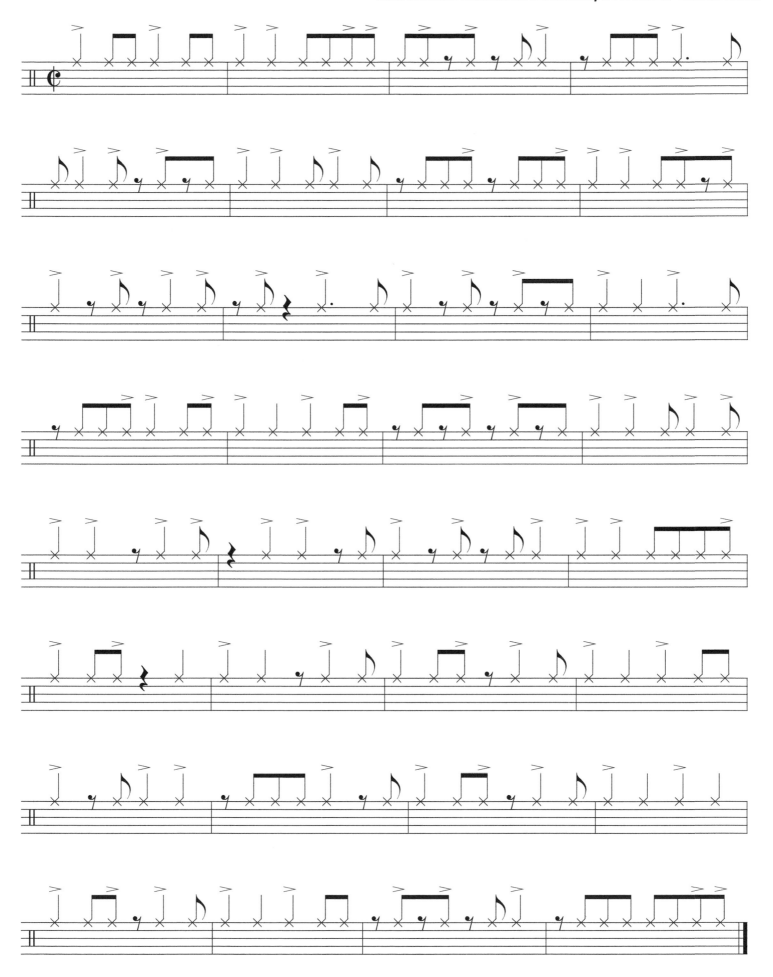

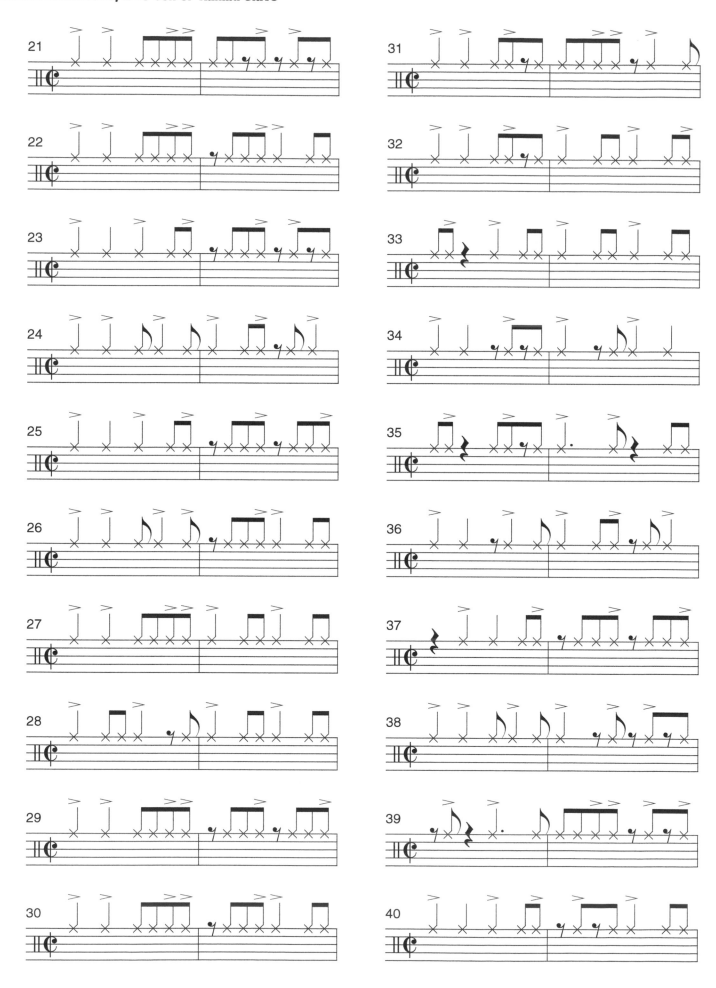

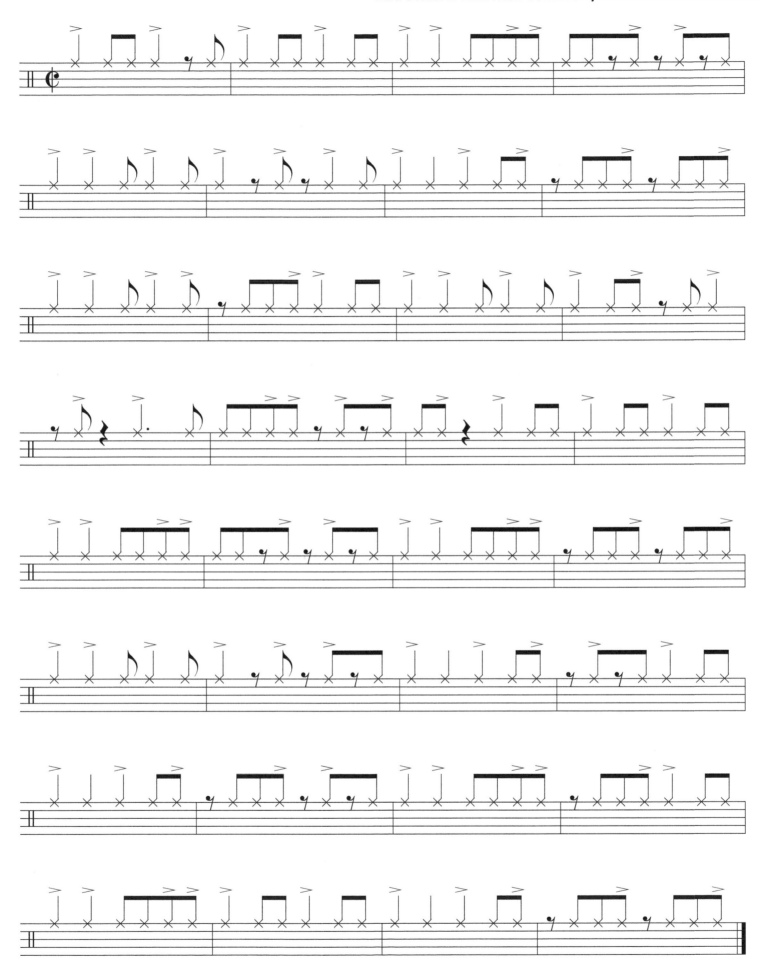

23

RIDE CYMBAL VARIATIONS, 3+2 Son or Rumba Clave

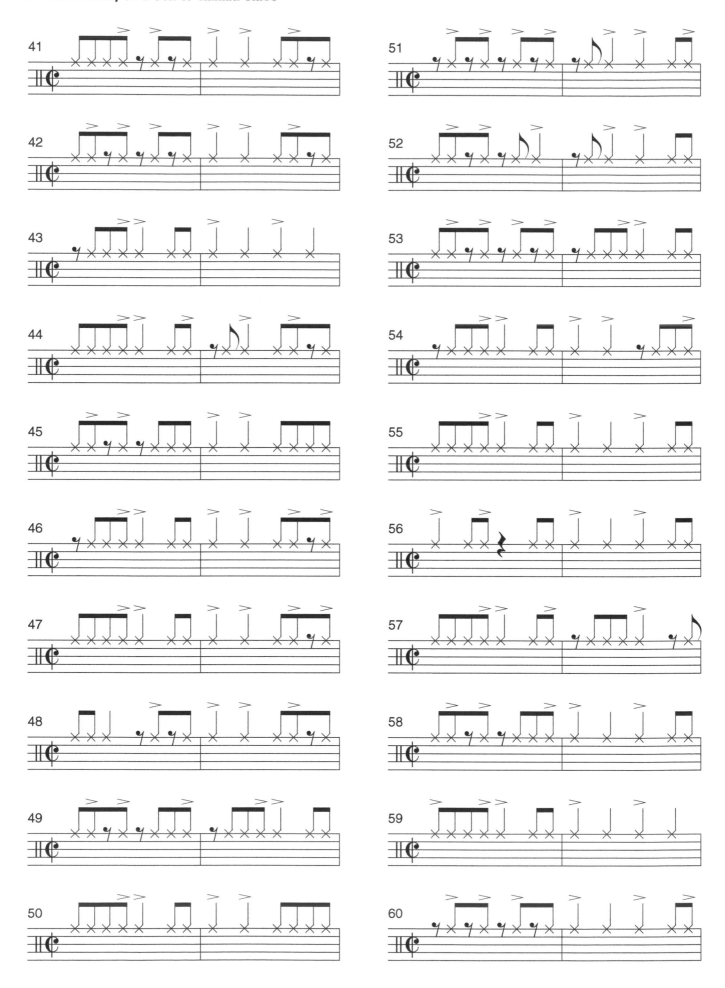

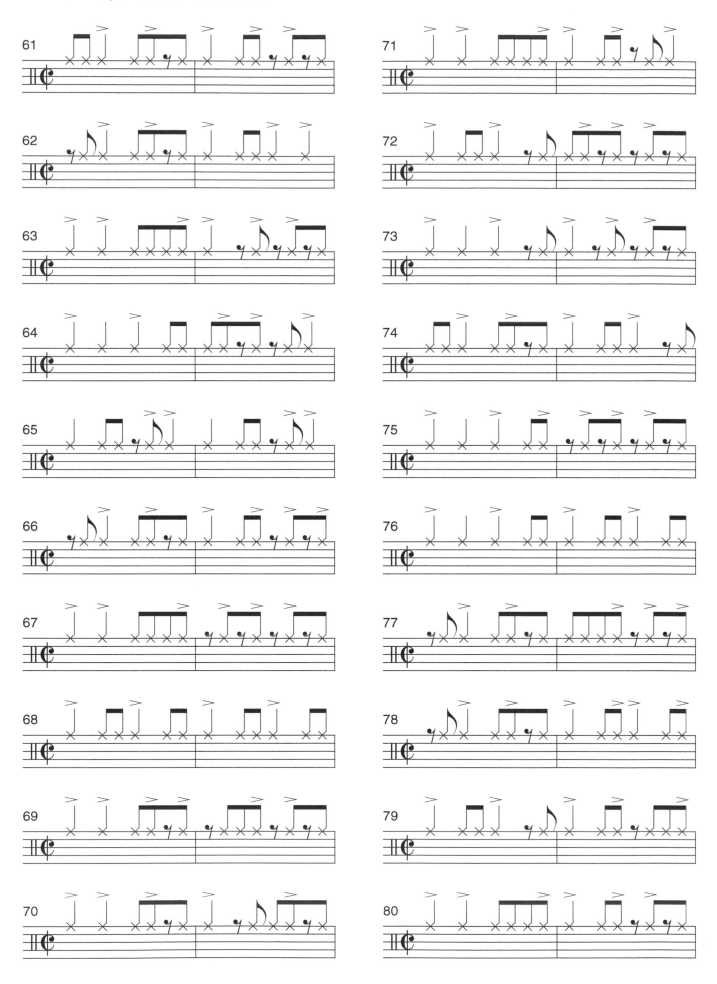

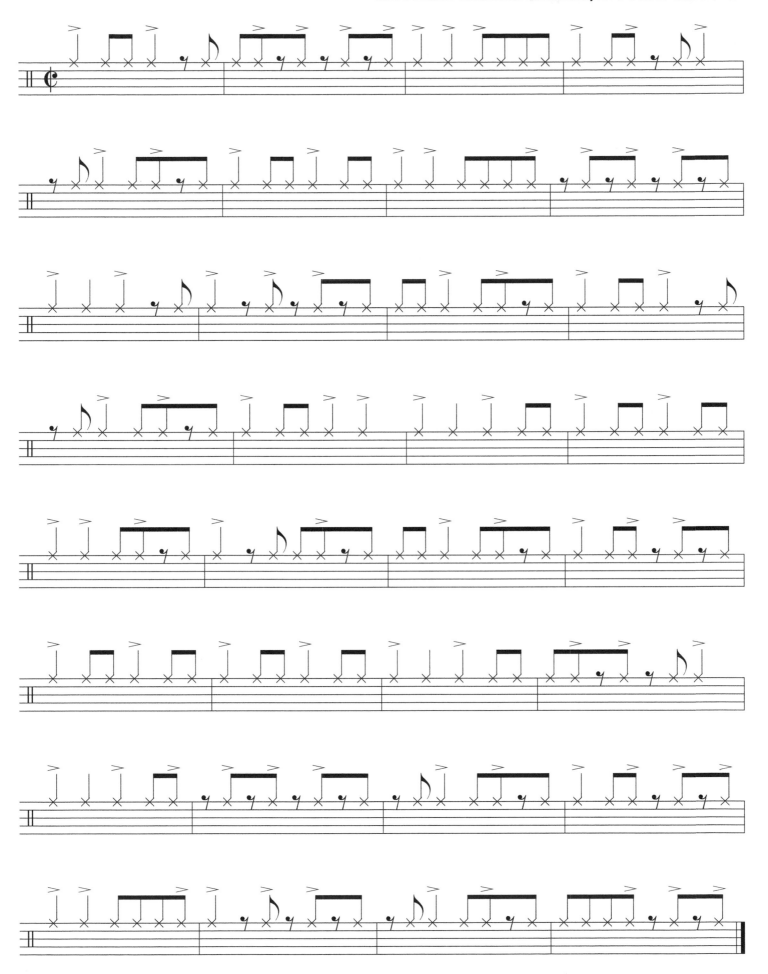

Chapter 3: LEFT-FOOT CLAVE

The following Mambo patterns feature the left foot maintaining the clave, which has become a popular technique in recent years. The left-foot clave can be played on the hi-hat pedal (as notated) or on a bass drum pedal mounted to a cowbell or Jam Block. As with the previous chapter, the left hand is playing a cross-stick snare drum note on the "and" of one in each cut-time bar, and a tom-tom note (or two) on the "and" of two. The standard cascara pattern is played on the ride cymbal or mambo bell. When using a mambo bell, play the accents on the open end of the bell and the other notes on the body of the bell.

Following these basic Mambo patterns are several pages showing ride cymbal (or mambo bell) variations in the four different clave feels. Because of the complexity of mastering the coordination, all of the parts from patterns 1, 2, 5 and 6 are shown in the corresponding variation examples so that you can see how the parts interact. (Patterns 3, 4, 7 and 8 each involve one additional tom-tom note, which can easily be incorporated once the variations are mastered with the patterns involving single tom-tom notes.) Typically, a drummer will play the standard two-bar cascara pattern during the A section of a standard AABA-style tune, and play a two-bar variation during the B section or "bridge." Variations are also frequently used during solo sections.

Begin by playing a pattern from this page and then play a two-bar ride cymbal (or mambo bell) variation, alternating between the two patterns. (Be sure that the clave patterns match when going between the patterns and the variations.) Individual lines from summary pages can be played as 4-bar phrases.

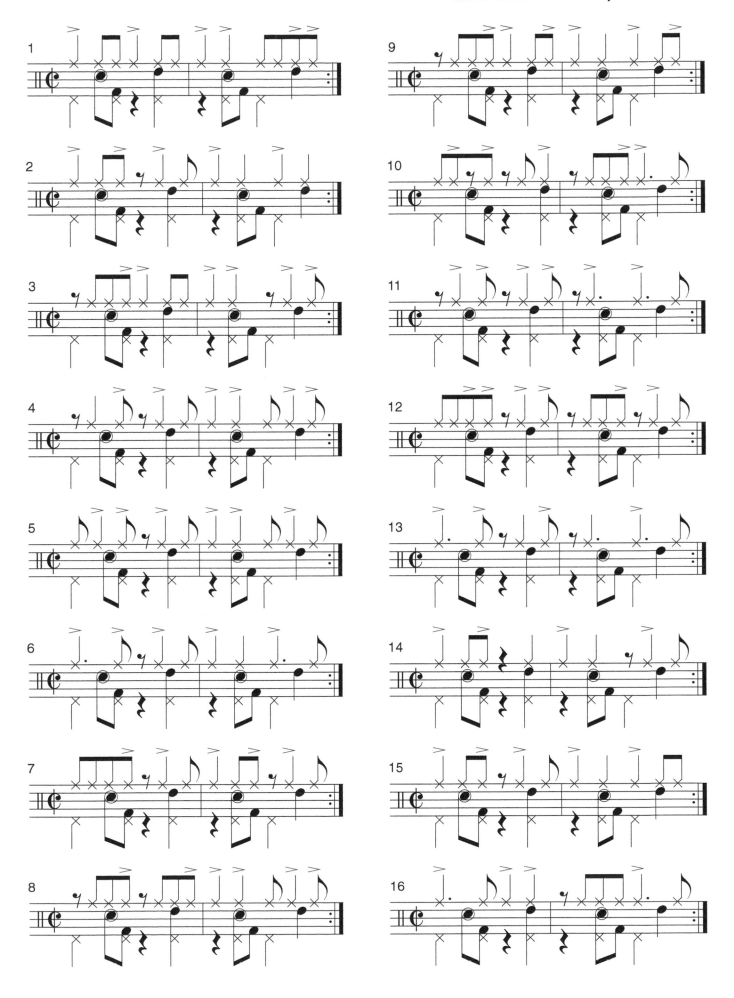

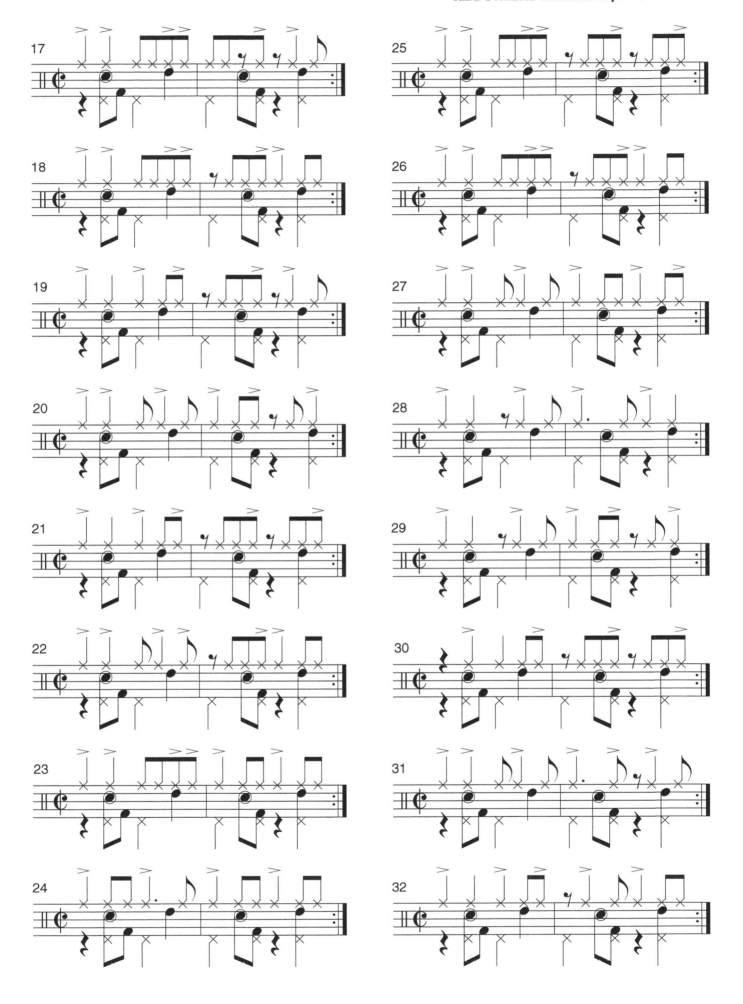

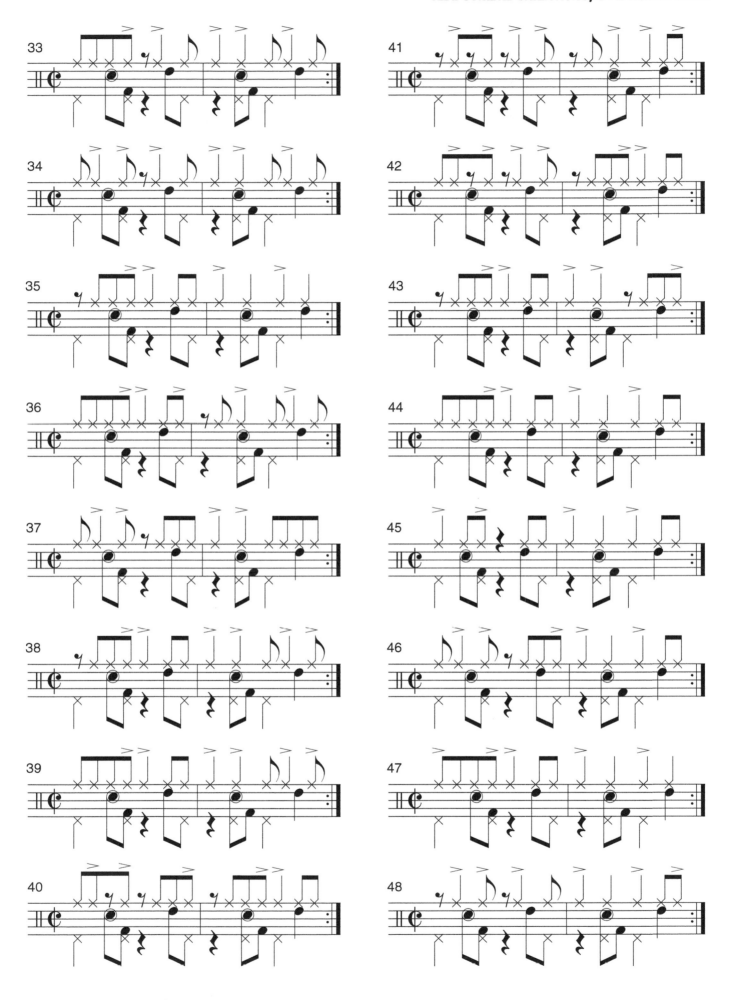

RIDE CYMBAL VARIATIONS, 2+3 Rumba Clave

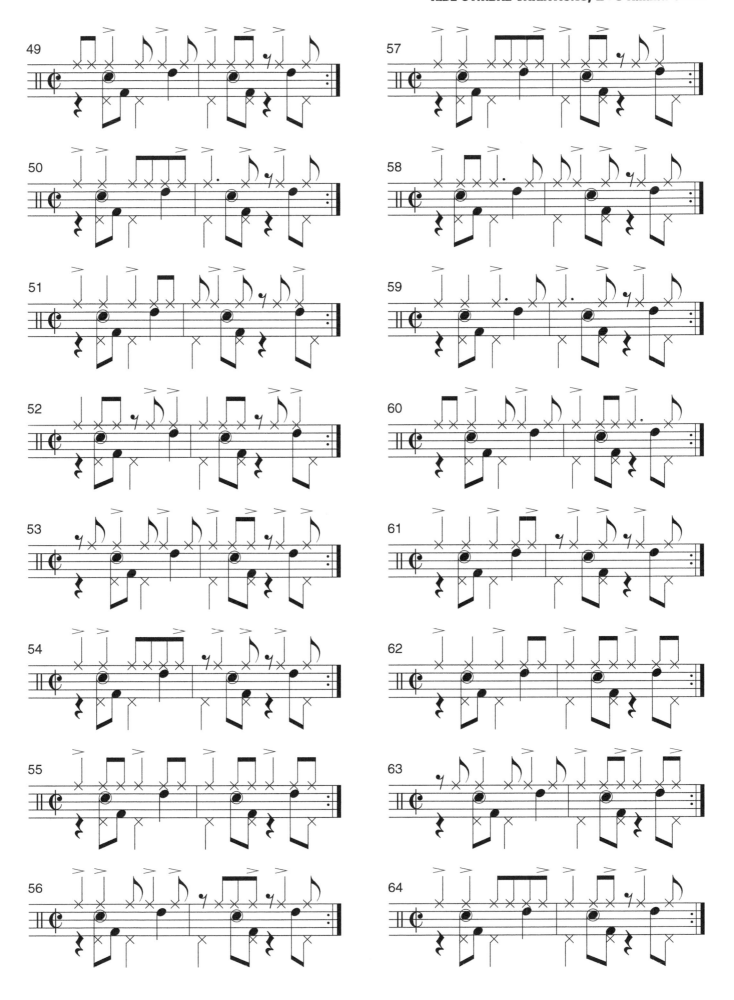

35

Chapter 4: BONGO-BELL OSTINATOS

The following Mambo ostinato patterns feature the right hand playing the pattern typically played on a cowbell by the bongo player in an Afro-Cuban ensemble during the dynamically loud or high montuno or mambo sections of a song. The ostinatos include variations for the bass drum and hi-hat, including left-foot clave on some patterns.

Following the page of ostinato patterns are several pages of variations and summaries showing an additional cowbell part that is to be played with the left hand. These rhythms correspond to the mambo-bell variations that would be played by the timbale player in an Afro-Cuban ensemble. Individual lines from the summaries can be played as 4-bar phrases.

On Latin-jazz tunes with an AABA structure, the drumset player should use the cascara pattern (as shown in Chapters 1, 2 and 3) for the A section. For the B or "bridge" section, instead of using one of the variations given in those chapters, you can use one of the patterns from this chapter.

Ideally, you should have two cowbells mounted on your drumset so that you can play the bongo-bell pattern with your right hand and the mambo-bell variations with your left hand. Play the left-hand rhythms in the center of the mambo bell in order to obtain a higher pitch.

3+2 Rumba or Son Clave

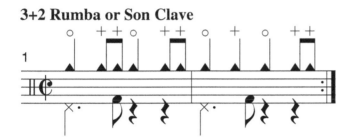

2+3 Rumba or Son Clave

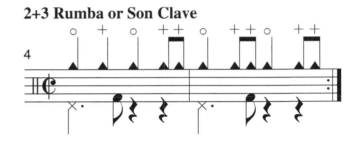

3+2 Rumba or Son Clave

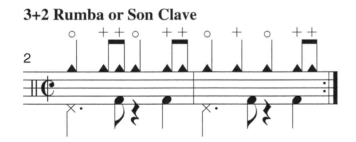

2+3 Rumba or Son Clave

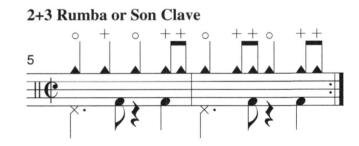

3+2 Rumba or Son Clave

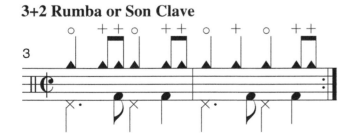

2+3 Rumba or Son Clave

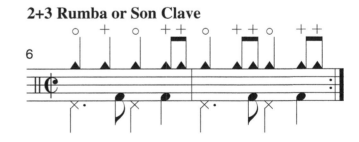

3+2 Rumba or Son Clave

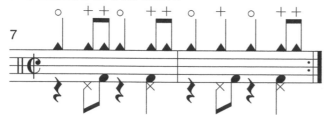

2+3 Rumba or Son Clave

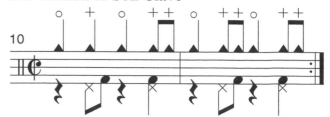

3+2 Son Clave

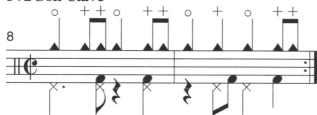

2+3 Son Clave

3+2 Rumba Clave

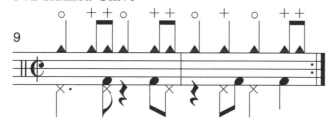

2+3 Rumba Clave

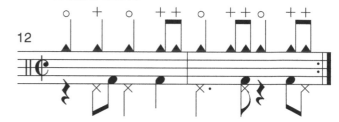

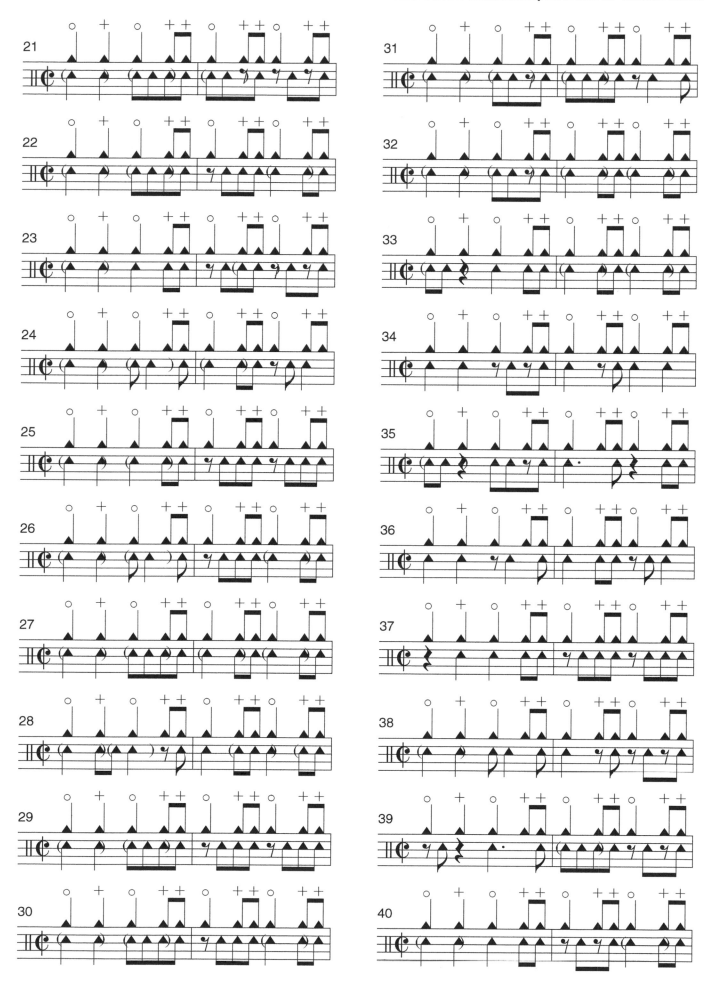

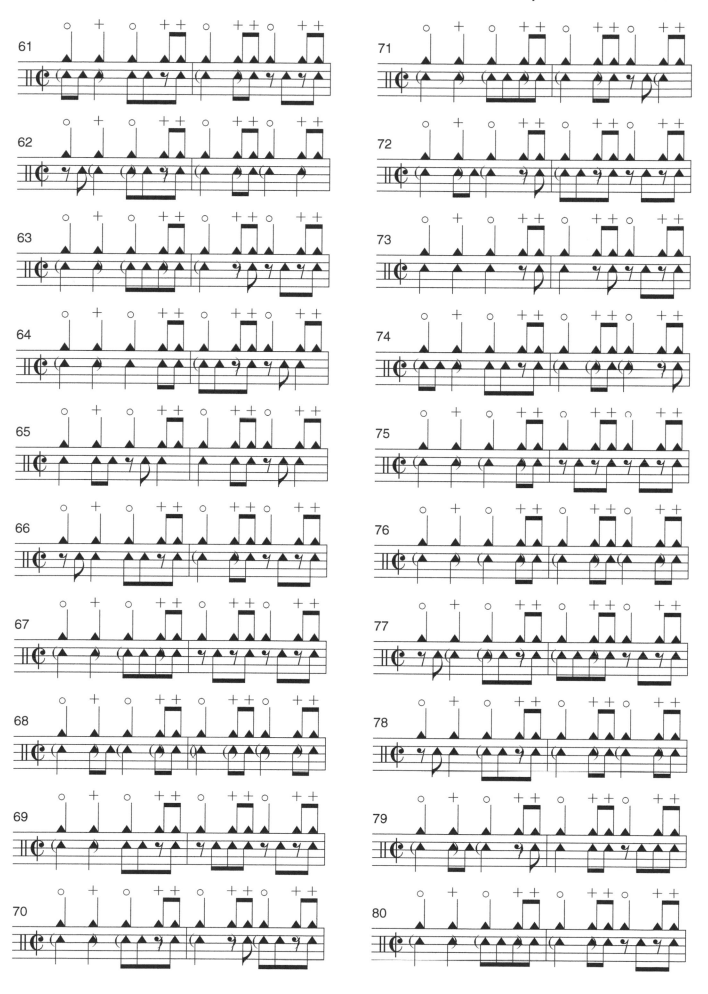

Chapter 5: IMPROVISATION

The following ostinatos feature the left foot playing rumba and son clave (3+2, 2+3) and the bass drum playing the tumbao figure. The ostinatos are shown in two versions: duple rhythms and triplets. In actual practice, they are often played identically, so that Afro-Cuban players can move in and out of duple and triple feels smoothly.

These ostinatos are to be used with the rhythm studies that follow, which are to be played hand-to-hand on snare drum and in unison (e.g., on ride cymbal and snare drum) along with the corresponding ostinato. The first section contains duple rhythms to be used with patterns 1–4, and that is followed by triplet patterns that can be played with ostinatos 5–8. Each section has its own summaries, and the chapter concludes with summaries that feature both duple and triplet rhythms. Individual lines from the summaries can be practiced as four-bar phrases. The goal is to be able to improvise and orchestrate your own musical rhythmic phrases over the ostinatos. All of the rhythm studies and summaries are notated with the 3+2 Rumba Clave to aid in the initial mastery of the coordination. To practice in 2+3 Rumba Clave, simply begin with the second bar of each rhythm study or summary. To practice in Son clave, only one note is different.

Once you feel comfortable with the mechanics of playing the rhythm exercises against the ostinato, orchestrate each exercise using the entire drumset (e.g., side of floor tom, cymbals, bells etc.). In order to further develop coordination, many of the patterns can be played with the right hand on ride cymbal or mambo bell in conjunction with the ostinatos in Chapters 1, 2 and 3. These rhythms, however, are not typical of the Afro-Cuban style, and are presented only for purposes of developing the necessary coordination that you can freely improvise in the Afro-Cuban style while maintaining left-foot clave.

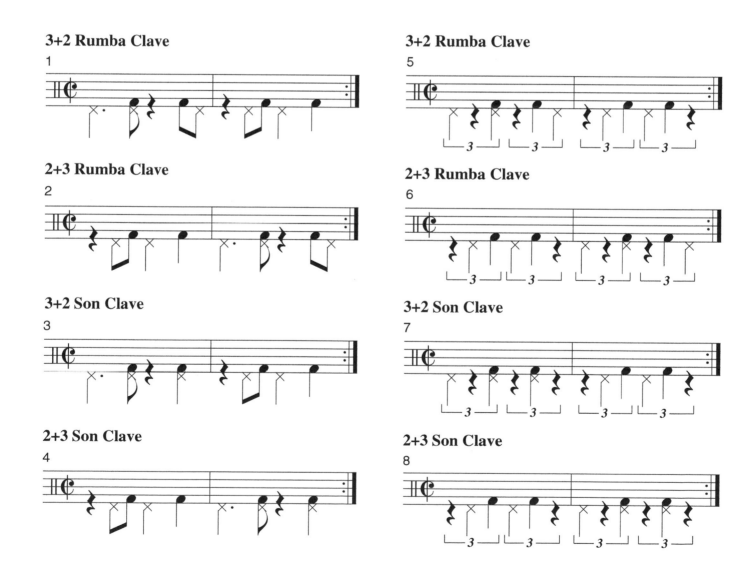

3+2 Rumba Clave
1

2+3 Rumba Clave
2

3+2 Son Clave
3

2+3 Son Clave
4

3+2 Rumba Clave
5

2+3 Rumba Clave
6

3+2 Son Clave
7

2+3 Son Clave
8

RHYTHM STUDIES, triplets

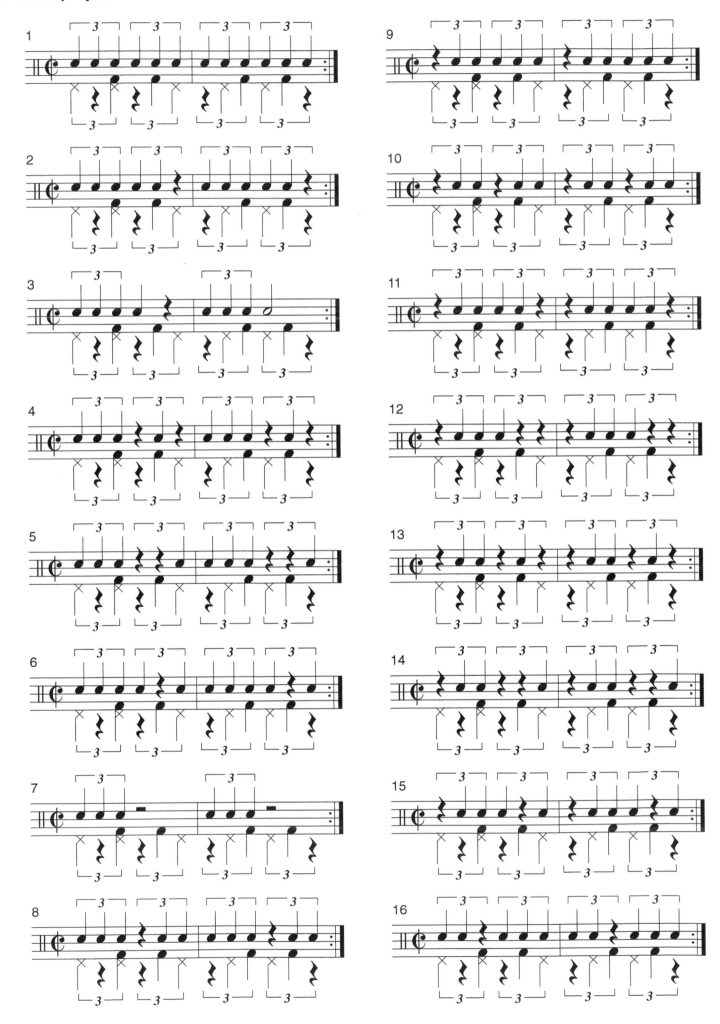

RHYTHM STUDIES, triplets

RHYTHM SUMMARY 4, comprehensive

Chapter 6: NANIGO

The Nanigo grooves shown below are derived from the percussion instruments that play the folkloric Cuban rhythm called Guiro, which is often played in religious ceremonies. The rhythm is traditionally played with sets of three or more shekeres (beaded gourds) and an iron bell. The Guiro style sometimes includes a tumbadora (low-pitch conga drum) or cajon (box).

The drumset has never been part of the traditional 6/8 Afro-Cuban style. But in the Latin-jazz style there are many different generic interpretations of the 6/8 Afro-Cuban rhythms, which are hybrids of the traditional Guiro rhythm and are sometimes referred to as Afro-Cuban 6/8 or Bembe. The Nanigo grooves written on this page are traditional drumset interpretations with a heavy emphasis on the dotted quarter note. These grooves work best during the melody or A section of a tune. The notated cowbell part can also be played on a ride cymbal.

The next page consists of bass drum variations in the Nanigo half-time feel. These grooves work best during instrumental or solo sections. The written snare drum parts include a heavy, accented backbeat (on beat one of the second bar), which implies the half-time feel. You should first practice these patterns without the ghost notes. The authentic bell pattern of the Nanigo rhythm can be played on a ride cymbal or cowbell. The final two pages of this chapter are summaries of the half-time bass drum variations, without the snare drum ghost notes. Individual lines of the summaries can be played as 4-bar phrases.

Practice going between the basic grooves shown on this page and the half-time grooves shown on the following pages. Play each groove an even number of times before making the transition to the half-time feel. First, play one groove from this page (and repeat several times); then play a half-time Nanigo feel from the next page. For a listening example refer to tracks 13, 15 and 17.

All of the patterns in this chapter can be played by substituting hi-hat for ride cymbal (or cowbell) and omitting the notated dotted-quarter-note hi-hat pulse played with the left foot.

NANIGO HALF-TIME VARIATIONS

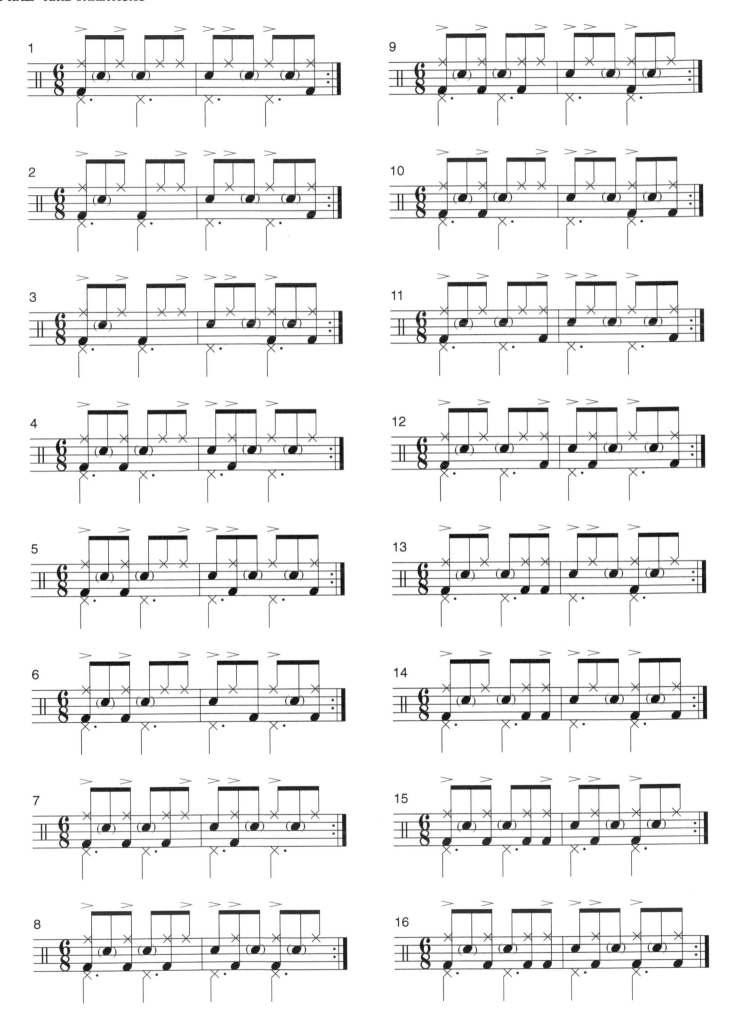

Chapter 7: SONGO

The Songo style of drumming is more of a concept than one particular "beat." Songo is a blend of folkloric and contemporary Cuban styles with elements of funk and jazz. In many ways, Songo is the "jazz" of Cuban drumming. Although there are many different ways to play Songo, the rhythmic style originated from approximately six to eight different grooves invented by Jose Luis Quintana, better known as "Changuito."

The Songo ostinatos written on this page are very popular grooves often played and heard in the "Latin-jazz" style of music. The next page features Songo ostinatos with left-foot clave patterns. The remaining pages in this chapter contain bass drum variations that can be played with the Songo ostinatos in order to develop the freedom and coordination to improvise bass drum patterns of your own.

Although the clave rhythm is not always played on the drumset, it plays an important role and it is important to always be aware of the clave while playing the Songo style. Although patterns 1–6 are only shown in 3+2 clave, they should all be practiced in 2+3 clave as well by starting on the second bar.

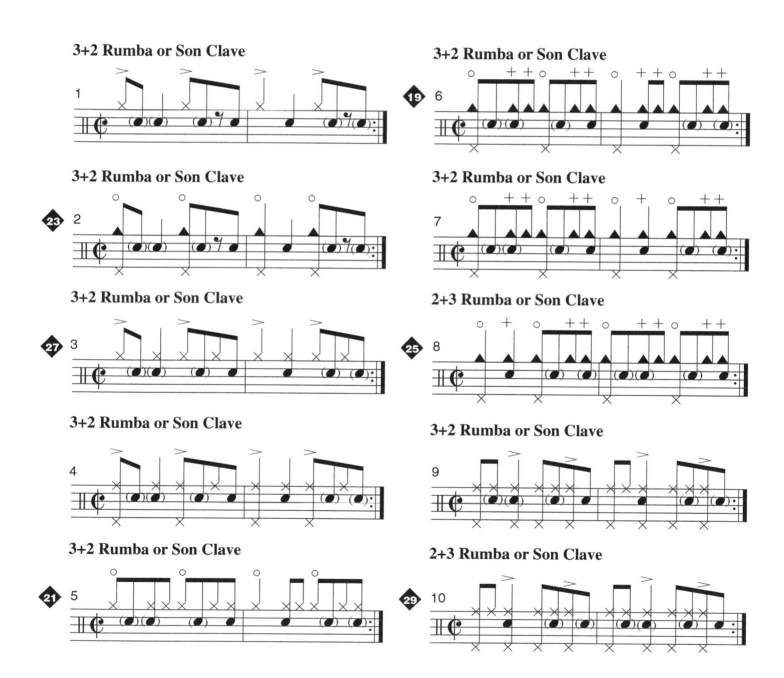

3+2 Rumba Clave

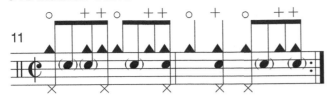

3+2 Son Clave

2+3 Rumba Clave

2+3 Son Clave

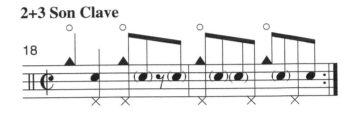

3+2 Son Clave

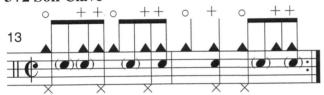

3+2 Rumba Clave

2+3 Son Clave

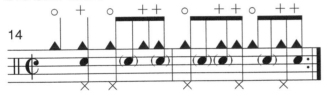

2+3 Rumba Clave

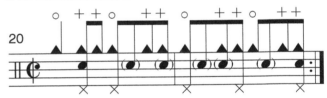

3+2 Rumba Clave

3+2 Son Clave

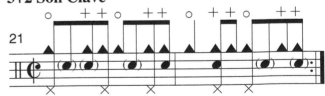

2+3 Rumba Clave

2+3 Son Clave

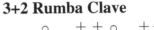

Chapter 8: MOZAMBIQUE

The Mozambique rhythm is traditionally a form of Carnival music from Cuba and was created in the 1960s by Pello Izquierdo, better known as Pello "El Afrokan." The traditional instrumentation consists of two cowbells (which are the signature sound of the Mozambique rhythm), two bass drums (high and low), three congas, horns (trombone), chorus and lead vocals. Later, timbales, percussion, electric guitar, and bass were added to the ensemble.

Although the drumset has never traditionally been part of the Mozambique style, the adaptations by many contemporary drummers has made the Mozambique popular, particularly with "Latin-jazz" bands. The grooves written on this page are more of a traditional approach for the drumset, and are written in 3/2 rumba clave (which is played with the cross-stick). Patterns 1 and 2 have the traditional high and low bass drum parts being played by the bass drum and with muted and open strokes on the floor tom. Patterns 3 and 4 include the cowbell parts that create the traditional sound of the Mozambique. These four patterns are all written in 3+2 Rumba clave, but they can also be played in 2+3 by starting on the second bar.

NEW YORK MOZAMBIQUE, 2-bar phrases

Contemporary Mozambique is sometimes referred to as "New York Mozambique" and is a hybrid of the traditional approach combined with elements of funk. The following pages contain a variety of bass drum variations that can be played with the New York Mozambique ostinato of ride cymbal (which plays the typical New York Mozambique cowbell part), snare drum, high tom, floor tom, and hi-hat with foot. Individual lines of the summaries can be played as 4-bar phrases. The New York patterns are all written in 2/3 clave, which is most common in contemporary Mozambique music. These are the patterns that are meant to be played with tracks 32, 34, and 36.

YOU CAN'T BEAT OUR DRUM BOOKS!

Bass Drum Control
Best Seller for More Than 50 Years!
by Colin Bailey
This perennial favorite among drummers helps players develop their bass drum technique and increase their flexibility through the mastery of exercises.
06620020 Book/Online Audio $17.99

The Complete Drumset Rudiments
by Peter Magadini
Use your imagination to incorporate these rudimental etudes into new patterns that you can apply to the drumset or tom toms as you develop your hand technique with the Snare Drum Rudiments, your hand and foot technique with the Drumset Rudiments and your polyrhythmic technique with the Polyrhythm Rudiments. Adopt them all into your own creative expressions based on ideas you come up with while practicing.
06620016 Book/CD Pack $14.95

Drum Aerobics
by Andy Ziker
A 52-week, one-exercise-per-day workout program for developing, improving, and maintaining drum technique. Players of all levels – beginners to advanced – will increase their speed, coordination, dexterity and accuracy. The online audio contains all 365 workout licks, plus play-along grooves in styles including rock, blues, jazz, heavy metal, reggae, funk, calypso, bossa nova, march, mambo, New Orleans 2nd Line, and lots more!
06620137 Book/Online Audio $19.99

Drumming the Easy Way!
The Beginner's Guide to Playing Drums for Students and Teachers
by Tom Hapke
Cherry Lane Music
Now with online audio! This book takes the beginning drummer through the paces – from reading simple exercises to playing great grooves and fills. Each lesson includes a preparatory exercise and a solo. Concepts and rhythms are introduced one at a time, so growth is natural and easy. Features large, clear musical print, intensive treatment of each individual drum figure, solos following each exercise to motivate students, and more!
02500876 Book/Online Audio...$19.99
02500191 Book...$14.99

The Drumset Musician – 2nd Edition
by Rod Morgenstein and Rick Mattingly
Containing hundreds of practical, usable beats and fills, *The Drumset Musician* teaches you how to apply a variety of patterns and grooves to the actual performance of songs. The accompanying online audio includes demos as well as 18 play-along tracks covering a wide range of rock, blues and pop styles, with detailed instructions on how to create exciting, solid drum parts.
00268369 Book/Online Audio................................$19.99

Instant Guide to Drum Grooves
The Essential Reference for the Working Drummer
by Maria Martinez
Become a more versatile drumset player! From traditional Dixieland to cutting-edge hip-hop, *Instant Guide to Drum Grooves* is a handy source featuring 100 patterns that will prepare working drummers for the stylistic variety of modern gigs. The book includes essential beats and grooves in such styles as: jazz, shuffle, country, rock, funk, New Orleans, reggae, calypso, Brazilian and Latin.
06620056 Book/CD Pack $12.99

1001 Drum Grooves
The Complete Resource for Every Drummer
by Steve Mansfield
Cherry Lane Music
This book presents 1,001 drumset beats played in a variety of musical styles, past and present. It's ideal for beginners seeking a well-organized, easy-to-follow encyclopedia of drum grooves, as well as consummate professionals who want to bring their knowledge of various drum styles to new heights. Author Steve Mansfield presents: rock and funk grooves, blues and jazz grooves, ethnic grooves, Afro-Cuban and Caribbean grooves, and much more.
02500337 Book..$14.99

Polyrhythms – The Musician's Guide
by Peter Magadini
edited by Wanda Sykes
Peter Magadini's *Polyrhythms* is acclaimed the world over and has been hailed by *Modern Drummer* magazine as "by far the best book on the subject." Written for instrumentalists and vocalists alike, this book with online audio contains excellent solos and exercises that feature polyrhythmic concepts. Topics covered include: 6 over 4, 5 over 4, 7 over 4, 3 over 4, 11 over 4, and other rhythmic ratios; combining various polyrhythms; polyrhythmic time signatures; and much more. The audio includes demos of the exercises and is accessed online using the unique code in each book.
06620053 Book/Online Audio...$19.99

Joe Porcaro's Drumset Method – Groovin' with Rudiments
Patterns Applied to Rock, Jazz & Latin Drumset
by Joe Porcaro
Master teacher Joe Porcaro presents rudiments at the drumset in this sensational new edition of *Groovin' with Rudiments*. This book is chock full of exciting drum grooves, sticking patterns, fills, polyrhythmic adaptations, odd meters, and fantastic solo ideas in jazz, rock, and Latin feels. The online audio features 99 audio clip examples in many styles to round out this true collection of superb drumming material for every serious drumset performer.
06620129 Book/Online Audio $24.99

66 Drum Solos for the Modern Drummer
Rock • Funk • Blues • Fusion • Jazz
by Tom Hapke
Cherry Lane Music
66 Drum Solos for the Modern Drummer presents drum solos in all styles of music in an easy-to-read format. These solos are designed to help improve your technique, independence, improvisational skills, and reading ability on the drums and at the same time provide you with some cool licks that you can use right away in your own playing.
02500319 Book/Online Audio...$17.99

HAL•LEONARD®

www.halleonard.com

Prices, contents, and availability subject to change without notice.

1221
022